Hoyden's Trove

Jane Newberry

hoyden /ˈhɔɪd(ə)n/ n. boisterous girl
The Little Oxford Dictionary, sixth edition.

First published by
Wheelsong Books
4 Willow Close,
Plymouth PL3 6EY,
United Kingdom

© Jane Newberry, 2022

The right of Jane Newberry to be identified as the author of this work has been asserted by her in accordance with the Copyright, Designs and Patents Act of 1988.

Cover art and illustrations © Jane Newberry, 2022

First published in 2022

All rights reserved. Except as permitted under current Legislation no part of this work may be photocopied, stored in a retrieval system, published, performed in public, adapted, broadcast, transmitted, recorded or reproduced in any form or by any means, without the prior permission of the copyright owners. Enquiries should be addressed to Wheelsong Books.

Print ISBN 979-8-40495-990-1

Be not afeard. The isle is full of noises, sounds, and sweet airs that give delight and hurt not. Sometimes a thousand twangling instruments will hum about mine ears, and sometime voices that, if I then had waked after long sleep, will make me sleep again. And then, in dreaming, the clouds methought would open and show riches ready to drop upon me, that when I waked I cried to dream again.

W Shakespeare.
The Tempest. Act 3, Scene 2.

For Pat – for ever

Acknowledgements

Thank you seems hardly enough for Martha Sprackland who believed in these verses while tutoring a weekend workshop at The Poetry School.

Equally I shall never forget a wild Cornish weekend with James Brookes editing further and convincing me I am a poet.

Meur ras Steve Wheeler - for crossing the border into Cornwall and being the most generous of editors.

Thank you to Laura, Joy, Summer and Holly for reading and to David Ishaya Osu for inspiring.

Love and thanks to all my wonderful family - your toils, tears and laughter went into the word-wash and came out as poems.

Contents

Acknowledgements	9
Foreword by Michael Morpurgo	13
Two Days	16
Small Hands	17
The Gift	18
Fractured	19
Holiday Fragment	20
Day of Bones	22
Fishing Jacket	24
Sunday Morning on the Mountain	26
Beach Café	28
Waking in Bloomsbury	30
Homage to Emily Hasler	31
On Finding a Rare Orchid	32
When David Read	34
Romance in Watercolour	35
Creek	36
Agaricus Campestris	38
Shaft of Light through Malcolm Mooney's Keyhole	40
Elegy for the Callington Unicorn	42
Lines Below the Bridge	43
Flowerman	44
The Falconer	46
Vignette: Potter Heigham	47
Strictly …	49
Community Singing	50

Michael's Old Terrier	52
A Passing Small Thing	53
Waiting for the Plague to Pass Over	55
Confrontation	56
Elizabeth	57
Survivor	58
Credits	61
About Wheelsong Books	63

Foreword

Every poem in this book is an invitation. Jane Newberry introduces us to her places, her people, her life.

To read them is to know her, to help us come to terms with our own familiarities. And every poem is a story, but a story best read aloud.

She makes poems that make music. These are the songs of her life. I hope they reach a wide audience. They most certainly should.

Michael Morpurgo

Two Days

of life bring a look of
elemental wisdom – unclouded
skin-touch perfection and I am
silent in awe at this perfectly-formed
being, sleeping yet wielding
such power.

Fragmentary moments of solemnity —
who knows what passes
across that sleep – invoking the
universal need to cradle,
to envelop sacred moments.

Here is Du Maurier's renewal of wonder
dawning of that terrifying dependence
till it dissolves, leaving us clinging,
resenting the unfamiliar identity
and looking back clouded by regret.

Look on, beyond — give way to
instinctive rocking, heart-beat pat;
indulge the fantasy in that
miraculous mirror image where
birth has removed the glass;
now is the moment for magi, shepherd …

or grandma.

Small Hands

My darlings have mastered clapping,
I make a sandwich
and they clap,
hide behind my dishcloth
and they clap.
I blow a bubble
and they applaud,
fingers spread, arms outstretched
full-on seal clapping.
unadulterated virgin spontaneity.
We cheer and join in
catching the shadow of elusive joy
loud clapping from the hollows
of old hands — skills we lose
so quickly and hide away in
pockets for awards and concerts.

The Gift

Was it the opening of the tin,
breathless shimmer of anticipation?
The lid displaying Derwentwater,
against a heaven of sky.
One small click and
lifting the tissue paper
I drank in the rainbow.
Every sharpened point the same;
no bitten ends or stumpy
odd men out and almost
too shiny to touch.
Most perfect of presents,
and had I that tin now
these margins would be
filled with grass and poppies,
worshipping a cadmium
yellow sun.

Fractured

A & E — 10.30 at night.
The doctor makes a bad start —
glancing at the wisp of humanity
clinging ever tighter round my neck;
"Why is he crying?"
The anger of incredulity
stems tears, while my silent
eyes say, "enter the world
of four-year-old
broken superheroes.

Doesn't he know about
Dr Evil-knees and
the giant hypodermic of doom?
and the X-ray machine which teleports
to another dimension?
And that saw for amputating
pirates' legs?
There's no bribing this guy with stickers
and bravery levels are
dangerously low.

"Just stop it hurting
I want to go home — "
and don't be surprised
if superheroes cry too.

Holiday Fragment

Cornish night in midsummer
when the dark is never really dark;
when you see your way
quite clearly and smell intensely
those scents of lemon balm and drains.
There I am again, in the
coastguard cottage dream,
drawn by the tang of seaweed
to an early morning swim,
transfixed by the steady oars of
fishermen catching the tide.
"When I row like that," I used to think.

But then it was sailing boats with
shale keels stuck in scraps of polystyrene
powered by seagull feathers.
Proudly gutting mackerel with
a new two-blade penknife, blue enamel
shining like a fish, shocking
innocents by throwing the guts
in where they paddle;
and the squelch of sodden
sand-daps all the way back
to the cottage; salt toes on the rush-mat
and diary writing by paraffin lamp.

Day of Bones

One

The perfect armour of spines
lay on the ground, unbuttoned, with
the sun-bleached ribs beside them
and the skull laughing a little,

eliciting no sadness, just surprise.
The skeleton crying graveyard and
death in that vibrant bower
with foxglove, campion and goat's beard
nodding urgently, vying for dominance.

Like an old memory gradually changing
with you – life and decay
juxtaposed tantalise the senses,
unsettling, when the mind shouts life
and art — turning away I lay a flower,
for remembrance.

Two

Light flashing in its eye
the fishbone sculpture
mocks me. Well, I could
criticise the rusty tips on
its rib bones if I chose;
who knows — I may outlast
the fish. How beautifully
the willow weaves between
the bones, as if the artist
planned to flesh the skeleton
that way. How accurately
the spine bends to the head
as if the fish were rising to
a fly. And will the rust,
willow and sun bleaching
the wooden head enhance
the art? And will I live long enough
to echo the quintessence?

Fishing Jacket

*You can't beat Donegal —
for a fishing coat*, he'd say,
and I would watch him unhook it
in the familiar satisfying way,
pocket bulging with pipe and pouch,
the square tin of hand-tied flies
wearing through the other
and elbow patches shiny —
faint smells evoking riverbank
and tobacco.

Base colours of peat bog,
essence of heather and sunlight pouring
from behind the Bluestack Mountains.
Way downhill the percussion of
shuttle and clacking of the
warping mill bring a chorus to that
grand opera of the wild places.

Singing raw ballads the weaver
remembers his knee-high boy
threading perns for pocket money.

Rare skills — beaming, slaying,
choosing your shuttle, so much art
before a jacket is born — born to last
and stem the chill, camouflaged
knee-deep in the river,

hues from those rows of bobbins,
all rippling in rich reflection.

Bent over the catch, he'd smile and say,
You can't beat Donegal.

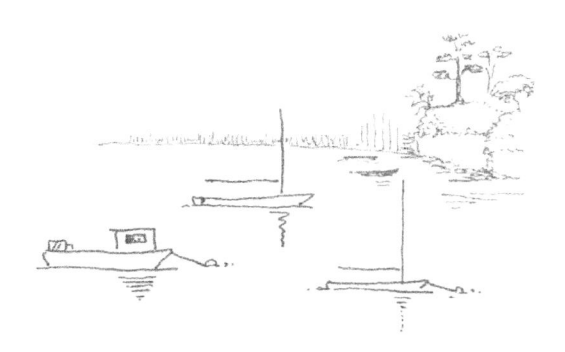

Sunday Morning on the Mountain

Unbelievable vast nothingness
hanging in that moment, enveloping,
leaving a desperate need to
compass and measure – to grasp
some boundary. Every sense
straining for a marker post to
gauge this overwhelming silence.

Somewhere traffic must be moving,
birds must be singing,
gates surely clanging
but as I bounce notions
across the void like a bat,
back it comes,
only nothing.

Unsettling, fearful almost
with no answer to my whispered
echoes and yet to break in
with a human utterance –
a cry, an oath, a song seems like
sacrilege, fracturing the
intangible web of silent mystery.

Even this high in the mountains
there is a road, a lane, a track,
and any moment a familiar
tractor will mark the end of my
held breath – but no rattle nor clank,
no buzzard nor raven,
no sheep coughing in the mist.
Could this be enchantment?

Wonder fights with fear,
catches in the throat,
upsets the step rhythm
and the unheard inward breath
pushing away the tiny seed
of thought that it happened
while I slept and
no-one else is left.

Beach Café

Speciality Coffee's
barista smoking by the door —
low season Marazion
less sand on the floorboards,
more steam to cloud the
view to the sea.

"panini and mozzarella?
crab salad?" — lightly distressed
pastel chairs and bunting,
neo-vintage, a few steps removed
from the old sardine-steeped town.
Ben's Bustin Burger — who is Ben?

Choose an emotion from
the specials board, wonder
which of the mouth-watering
ice cream flavours are left the
wrong side of September.
A wolfhound parks its nose
on the table — no-one notices.

"Wedges and a milk shake?" —
the corner artist too deep
in her dreams to look up,
vague folksy music changes key
and begs the world's forgiveness.

"Wedges anyone….?"

A faded surfing poster curls and drops,
"Prawn mayo on brown…?"
Sun silvers the sea
between the showers —
not long till closing time.
"sauces are all in the bucket".

Waking in Bloomsbury

Glad Bulgarian builders, loud and reassuring
clanking scaffolding beyond the glass,
breaking through the hamster-cage artifice
of that Bloomsbury hotel.

Alien plastic bed — predictable pictures,
choice of pillows, galaxy of herbal teas —
so many cushions, smothering and jeering;
pitying mirrors too bland and clean.

Searching for reality beyond the window —
one builder had a baby only yesterday
one was in fight last night and
one is singing, of going home.

Depth in that snatch of song, unlike
the snow-white slippers which are not mine.
Now, a tired child, I want *real* slippers,
grubby, squashed slippers,
where my feet belong.

Homage to Emily Hasler

"Someone with pockets like that
must be a poet!" she said,
and she a real poet, of distinction.

Not just anyone; me — a someone,
with two symbolic muses.
I thought my head would explode

with excitement; did I sound
squeaky? — Voices ebbed and flowed
as I pondered the concept, —

not one, but two ... and
stepping around the bent tube ticket,
old Immodiums, shredded

tissue and three sea shells,
who knows what might germinate
in those poetic pockets?

On Finding a Rare Orchid

Collective noun for bluebells?
exquisite Wedgewood carpet,
— a drift, a wealth, an intensity?

Stiff breeze subtly changing
tones as each stem dances
to the wind's gutsy tune.

Hard to stay in the doldrums
surrounded by the blue;
why is it called the blues . . .?

For here they lift me up
and then — this refugee princess —
an orchid I had never seen,

tiny florets of intense deep purple,
piled pyramid of decadence
looking tropical and un-British

with serpentines and hoods
evoking rich silk designs
from the Ottoman empire,

shy foreigner among the brassy bluebells
and I must cup the floral head in my hand,
protect this specimen from the gale,

trust memory to unlock the image
like a Russian icon on darker days —
keep that imperial hue in my mind's eye.

Fold exotic spotted leaves
around you and sleep safely
princess.

When David Read

Courtier-like he sat on the sofa,
not of our mundane world,
fingering his notebook
while all around hung rich
echoes — *quinquireme of nineveh*.
When he read I said
"what comes between
a poem and a song?"
Spreading the syllables like
honey, those words his own,
sifted from his father's library,
honed in the lonely places
and intoned with magic, eyes
alive with the possibility of
wonder. Words cloaking me
with warmth like sweet liqueur,
such depth and colour melting
through me, all on the edge
of tears — when David read.

Romance in Watercolour

I always wanted to capture the sea
with that tin box, chink-chink
of the brush and jam-jar
questions from the Newlyn school
and answers snatched by the wind

great sweeps of foam
tickle and drown
so many unsuitable shoes
and the gulls' mocking laughter
all the louder
breathe free tumble toss

pebbles sucking muffling voices
thump and release
perplexing the artist's
method and eluding the
brush — *thou shalt not*
paint the smell of seaweed
and the hidden places.

But I do see them —
their flying manes
while along the ledge
caramel kelp wafts
with the tide hypnotic
and velvet down below
whispering *come.*

Creek
Restronguet

You can't go back, and yet I do…to dream
about the would, and should,
the path to
                         might have been
and by the creek as ebb tide turns to flood
subconscious drift to relish solitariness — and mud.

Waders call long summons, cutting through
                                  the peace
and swans, great messengers from the gods
                                  release
the tension of their flight; webbed feet cut
                                  mirror calm
with ripples spreading ever on in waves
                                  of pure soul balm.

As every minute leaves more mud exposed —
                that elemental creek-side smell;
my senses shrink, but then remember,
yes — all is
well
and fishermen still move from tenders, unhurriedly
                                  to larger boats,
unsung enduring mastery of a lifetime spent afloat.

Perched high on my rock where oak trees
                              cleave the shore

I'm free to dream — to be a child once more,
exploring tidal margins and hearing acorns thud
to break the reflected silence that guards this
                              world of mud.

Agaricus Campestris

No-one understands mushrooms,
spellbinding and timeless
defying this misty, drizzling morning —
dewy, damp tracks left in the field
to betray the places where
prized treasure nestles in the grass.

Sense of wonder is still the same
as mushroom mornings years ago,
setting out with willow baskets
and that odd glup-glup noise
that bare legs make in gumboots —
younger eyes scanning the ground.

No surprise that myth and magic
wound round still foggy mornings
like this – *fairies only grant
mushrooms to really good people,*
she said and I would tense my
body and renew the hunting effort.

Still the thrill, still the excitement —
the surprise when you find it
all pearly snow-white, and reverence
and delicacy govern the picking,
an upending check revealing the
softest pink feather-strand gills

and the smell that is mushroom —
no need really for the third check,
the peeling, for the scent is hypnotic,
bringing back countless past hunts
and for an indulgent moment
plunging me deep in a sensory limbo

Shaft of Light through Malcolm Mooney's Keyhole

I add my song to love
hoping it will be enough
to fill that space to the edges

for what lurks in the little
  gaps   in between
and unchecked pushes
at the boundaries.

No one needs the
passport to that asylum
where weird discordant
music plays on emotions

with chromatic rising
atonal splitting then
sighs with some growing sense
of descending and relief

abstracting to the elementals

> *feel fire*
>   *cleanse water*
>   *sand filters through fingers*

gently tipping the scale
to platonic orgasm.

Speaking in silence to the
soul spirit in the here and now.

Too wondrous to marvel
in frozen wasteland;
too wasted yet marvellous
    to wonder.

Elegy for the Callington Unicorn

I never thought to see
a dead unicorn,
but there it was.
Hung itself on the fence,
futility distilled —
burst, under the burden
of dreams.
Drabness beyond tears.
Myth, mystery and magic
deflated and dissolved
in a puff of stale air, and
was that once-proud horn
simply an illusion?
Now the image flaps
and fades
like paper in the rain.

Lines Below the Bridge

Venturing out in Saltash —
Is this how they felt after Chernobyl?
Everything a little unreal,
certainty provided by the Co-op,
still turquoise, still shabby,
still there and, by the waters' edge
where salt-laden gales wash
the benches, the man from the
Council is doing it again
and mowing the daisies,
the pretty end of town.

Daringly buying coffee,
real cappuccino,
sandwiched between the vet and
the barber, time stands still
at Bella's Coffy — gangsta pirates
of yesteryear still hanging,
unchanged by Covid.
Yet Saltash is still Saltash,
sleeping in pandemic coma,
still bathed in a glow of inconsequence
with nothing much to sell and
carpet-slippered old folk
shambling nowhere.

Flower Man

Every year on Valentine's Day
I get a fit of sadness.
It comes through the open door
with the Interflora man —
because I want you now and
won't be distracted like a small child.
My tantrum's real and I take it out
on the packaging, spearing the tape
with scissors and plonking the poor stems
in an uninspiring vase —
all those layers of cellophane
and artificial tissue,
insulation for emotion
so it can't get out.

And if you were really shopping
what would you choose?
Do you see me in pinks,
chrysanthemums or roses?
I just want the half-price saddos
from the supermarket
or garage flowers,
wilting gently, — in your hand
bringing you home
framing your face

or daffodils from a roadside
honesty box

The Falconer

Across the narrow street
I saw the falconer.
Nonchalant on the cobbles
in defiance of the era.
Same gauntlet, hood and jesses,
sure in his skill; unchanged
since others like him charmed
the Sultans of the Alhambra,
where chill winds from the Sierra Nevada
now shift ghostly spirits
in the empty halls.
Through half-closed eyes and cryptic lattices
see the conquering hero, Fernando of Aragon
smiling triumphant at Isabella and
banishing the last Nasrid ruler Boabdil
from his cherished Alhambra.
Moorish dynasty beaten to submission,
and yet what lasts?
In unchanged Albaicín streets
lined gipsy faces keep truths older
than the patterns on the tiles.
Who shall stride across
the barriers of time? —
the falconer.

Vignette: Potter Heigham

Across the river
from my moored boat
I watch them,
like a spy, although
if they could see me
they would not care.

He's on his fishing stool;
she stands close by;
she's of an age when
everything droops.
He is baiting her hook,
a slow process to tease
the tough end of the
maggot on the tip.

They're not speaking,
bathed in the June heat,
bound in the intensity
of the moment.
Slowly and painfully
he stands and casts her line
just a little way, and
checks it to bob the float.

She takes her rod from him
and, slumping into her
canvas chair, she settles,
reaches out,
and holds his hand.

Strictly …

It was only a short clip
in their Penzance front room,
crowded round by books and photographs.
She, sitting at the piano, plays

in a jaunty staccato; he dances
beside her, a little unsteady perhaps,
but infected by the rhythm, adding a gesture,
singular odd panache, swaying

in his favourite cardi, giving it his all,
joy bursting through the wrinkles
until she rallentandoes expertly
to the final notes; he sings out of tune

and hugs her very lightly, laughing.
She smiles. Bravo and encore for
sharing something so precious.
Then the message on the screen

says they were over eighty and
had dementia — had dementia?
had a depth of love,
a talent forever,

and I turned up the volume
and played it over again, and
relishing the eruption of
pleasure inside me,
I played it yet again.

Community Singing

"It'll do you a power of good, Mrs P —
It won't matter that you can't sing."

Oh but it will; the pain will sear
my soul, don't you see?

For she has closed the box
on the girl who played
Stockhausen on the piano,
who sat up half the night
finding the sound.

She who leaned forward in the
front row at Aldeburgh,
swept up in the newness,
moonstruck.

Glorious corruption of innocence,
atonal fireworks
and the great choral works,
pushing the boundaries at Dartington,
breaking the mould again and again.

Fast forward the years of Wexford Festivals,
Prussia Coves and Glyndebourne.

    Like a lightning flash
     the stroke broke the music
      and the rebel spirit
       in one day of hell.

What is a thrush without song?
What use one hand grieving
for a lost partner?
Sighs replace the agile footstep
hurrying across the bridge to
the Festival Hall.

If I could end it all you know I would.
"Oh don't let's talk like that".
But it is written in the notes,
while the trolley comes around
with cake and tea.

Michael's Old Terrier

Empty patch of sunlight
outside the cottage on the lane
where Michael's dog was always there.

Three stiff legs, one tucked up;
a sideways flap, one ear steeple-tall;
those cloudy eyes kept sentry there.

Defined by that tail, wagging for Michael
as silently they filled the ritual hour;
a comfort of necessity out there.

I'll have to do it; — I'll know the time,
hastening the end, too hard to bear,
the thought of that small dog not being there.

A Passing Small Thing

I can see us now
standing in the churchyard
emotion still fermenting
just under the surface.
The vicar tousled, with his
surplice billowing in
the February blast.
Basic tools of spade,
fork and sympathy to hand
and the naked rose bush.

There we poured everything
into that earthy hole
with hidden birds
composing the requiem.
Anger mixed with bitterness;
sorrow; bewilderment;
exhaustion and pain
crumbled in the planting
and the prayers followed
and the rose bush trembled.

Treading the plant, silent ritual;
we stand there hoping for
the caress of caring
but the wind merely whispers
through riven spaces between.
Later, deer ate the bush
and then we knew that
nothing is for ever — marking
baby's loss no more constant
than the leaves on the trees.

Waiting for the Plague to Pass Over

Do not let fear seep beneath the door.
Swaddled by the golden warmth of love
we need not paint the blood on thresholds any more

or kneel to kiss the earth upon the floor,
protection paid for with a pair of doves,
do not let fear seep beneath the door.

Ancient rituals steeped in visceral gore
have all been superseded from above,
we need not paint the blood on thresholds any more,

yet creeping plague infects both rich and poor —
new rituals, priests with visors, gowns and gloves;
do not let fear seep beneath the door,

and no escape to distant hill or moor
to sanctuaries where the tortured soul seeks salve;
we need not paint the blood on thresholds any more.

Upturned faces waiting for the jug to pour
blest unction making us immune and tough,
do not let fear seep beneath the door —
we need not paint the blood on thresholds any more.

Confrontation

Today my hair arrived in a box.
I broke open the package curiously,
a white box, giving nothing away.
The lid lifted and a single sheet of tissue
revealed the hair, trapped in a net.
Very prim; no kin to my unruliness
and I stared at it, transfixed

as it defined the state of things,
the outward face to the world
the real mirrored image
the pallid spectre
that disquiets and shocks
and sends folk to the
other side of the street.

That face will do; that scarred
gladiator is my friend; those
last wisps, survivors of the torture
stand proud, like ragwort on the hill
and I quietly replace the lid
on the anonymous
white box.

Elizabeth

In exams they used to call "*Elizabeth . . .*"
she didn't answer for a long time.
"Who the hell's Elizabeth?" they wondered.

The name was never used,
it never fitted.
It languished in officialdom.

Still smarting from Ma's
"plain Jane and no nonsense" she
dreamt her way through middle age.

She actually wanted to be Joe —
treasured a penknife for years,
climbed trees and went fishing.

Picture the grim bridesmaid.
Never was anyone so angry and
affronted in garlands and pink.

After all the years, it matters little.
Jane digs spuds and battles brambles,
Elizabeth's hospital number is F716333.

Survivor

Now I know how wonderful
a Great War hero was.
He'd been to Ypres and kept his story
tight; just that shrapnel bump
above the chair, swathed in smoke
from Guards cigarettes.

Quiet, understated driving style
leaving with a little spurt of gravel
and mackerel — he shook them
off the hook with one practised hand,
whacked to stun and in the box. —
No one ever said *disabled.*

Only later, when he'd gone
we found the pictures; debonair
young man in uniform with a
far-away look, son and soldier
— stranger to the old man
with the tic and shrunken hand.

No-one spoke of shell-shock
or the war.
All too raw and packed away
with letters in old ammo crates.
The survivor brought chocolate,
smoked, and watched the sea.

Credits

All images and artwork
© Jane Newberry 2022

Book design and layout
© Steve Wheeler 2022

Poems first appeared in the following publications:

South Poetry - Small Hands, South 62 October 2020

RedWolf Editions - Waiting for the Plague to Pass Over
Under the Bridge
Coronavirus Anthology September 2021

Acumen Literary Journal - Agaricus Campestris January 2022

Used with permission

About Wheelsong Books

Wheelsong Books is an independent publishing company based in Plymouth, on the beautiful South West coast of England.

Established by poet Steve Wheeler in 2019, the company aims to promote unheard voices and encourage new talent in poetry. Wheelsong is also the home of the Absolutely Poetry anthology series, featuring previously unpublished and emerging poets from around the globe.

You can read more about Wheelsong Books and its growing stable of exciting new poets on the website:

www.wheelsong.co.uk

Printed in Great Britain
by Amazon